Christmas Card Magic

THE ART OF MAKING
DECORATIONS AND ORNAMENTS
WITH CHRISTMAS CARDS

By the Same Author

CHRISTMAS MAGIC
THE ART OF MAKING
DECORATIONS AND ORNAMENTS

Christmas Card Magic

THE ART OF MAKING
DECORATIONS AND ORNAMENTS
WITH CHRISTMAS CARDS

Margaret Perry

PHOTOGRAPHS AND DRAWINGS
BY THE AUTHOR

Doubleday & Company, Inc., Garden City, New York
1967

LIBRARY OF CONGRESS CATALOG CARD NUMBER 67–19802
COPYRIGHT © 1967 BY MARGARET PERRY
ALL RIGHTS RESERVED
PRINTED IN THE UNITED STATES OF AMERICA
FIRST EDITION

CONTENTS

LIST OF COLOR ILLUSTRATIONS

INTRODUCTION

When a Christmas card has been selected, signed and sent it has completed half its mission. When it has been received and read, and then placed among the holiday tributes, its mission is accomplished.

At the end of the holiday season, perhaps on Twelfth Night, when the Christmas cards are taken down along with the other decorations, they are once more read and admired and then tossed away. The card has carried its message, it has maintained for one more year the tenuous thread of friendship and goodwill, it has done its job and can now be disposed of.

But what a treasure house those Christmas cards are! A wealth of color, design, pattern, infinite variety of figures and fantasy. And each of these treasures is created with care on paper of particular size, weight, and texture. A quick run through your Christmas cards will disclose an assortment of materials from gold to green and from tissue to weighted foil, an assortment impossible to assemble otherwise without a wide, wide search.

9

With a pair of scissors and a pot of paste this storehouse of treasures can be transformed into villages, crèches, mobiles and mats, carousels, candle ruffs and candy containers, coasters and posters, and centerpieces for parties the whole year round.

Don't toss away your treasures. Tuck them away, and when the next stormy day arrives let the children help you conjure up creations for next year's Christmas tree and next summer's birthday parties. Make use of this rich assortment of colors and shapes, and be ready for the holidays when the season comes around again.

1

For This Year and Next

FOR EACH OF US the holiday season begins when the first Christmas card arrives. Weeks before Christmas Eve we start our collection of cards—a colorful collection that brings us good wishes from friends and family at home and abroad.

This first bright manifestation of the Season of Light heralds the holidays and sets the mood of the season. If you display your colorful collection of Christmas cards where you and your friends can enjoy them, you will catch the spirit of the festivities to come.

CHRISTMAS CARD TREE

Brightly colored or plainly gold, intricately designed or severely simple—each Christmas card brings a message expressed in design and words, and each one is different. We all have our favorite ways of displaying this bounty of Christmas cheer and making it part of our holiday decorations. Here's one way that is easy and effective and just right for the hall table, a welcoming burst of color.

Dried branches are sprayed white or gold and set in plaster of Paris in a coffee can. The plaster is simple to prepare—just add water until you have a doughlike mixture. Place the branches in the coffee can full of plaster as you want them to stay, and hold them in place for a few minutes until the plaster begins to set. In about ten minutes it will harden, and your tree is ready to use.

Cover the coffee can with bright paper, or spray it with red or gold paint (or a color to match your decor). Trim top and bottom edges with strips of gold beading cut from last year's Christmas cards. Attach with glue.

Fasten the cards to the tree with small strips of cellophane tape—don't make holes in the cards or you might destroy next year's decorations!

As the days go by and more cards arrive, add them to the tree. It will hold many more than you would think possible, and all of them can be easily seen.

THE CARDS YOU WANT TO KEEP

What do you do with your very special Christmas cards, the artistic creations you cannot part with, the cards that are rare and must be carefully preserved?

Such cards are treasures indeed, not to be treated merely as holiday greetings but cherished through the years.

One set of unusually lovely Christmas cards, drawn by Artist John Groth, hangs in the hallway of some friends of mine, framed all alike. Done professionally in a local shop, the frames vary in size according to the card. The group of pictures dominates the entrance hall.

No glass is used. The cards are mounted on blocks of wood set in deep wood frames that are black edged with antique gold. One can see at a glance that the

drawings are all done by the same artist, but the subjects range from Christmas family scenes to the journey of the Magi on their camels.

A New York art director who, because of his profession, receives many distinctive cards, finds it difficult to keep them all and yet cannot part with them easily. He and his wife have found a solution—they choose, by a vote, the finest one of the year. That one card is then framed and added to their growing collection on the wall of their recreation room. The frames for these cards are all alike too, a narrow antique white.

Some other friends of mine, who have an artist in their family and always find their Christmas mail filled with lovely cards, hang their choicest ones on their Christmas tree.

Reproductions of the works of famous artists are often used for greeting cards. These can be preserved, as pictures or for reference. One way is to group several together or use them singly in the popular glass frames available at art supply shops—the frames that consist of two pieces of glass held together with metal clips. If you keep a boxful of your especially fine cards, you can make a change from time to time. It is easy to accomplish with this type of frame.

GIFT TAGS AND GIFT CARDS

Perhaps you have at one time or another made Christmas gift tags out of Christmas cards. But to make tags that are professional-looking, in proper proportion, with illustrations in the right sizes, takes a little extra thought and time.

The best cards for making tags are those made of double paper. These usually have tiny illustrations on the inside of the card opposite the message. Sometimes it is a duplicate of the larger illustration on the front of the card.

This tiny inside illustration can usually be folded and

cut out with an oblong-shaped piece of the card in such a way that there will be no writing on the inside of your newly made tag.

The final touch—but an important one—is the hole through which to slip the tag's string. If you use a punch the tag will look neat and professional. Use gold cord

or use red string for tying the tag to the package.

As gift cards without strings, these tiny cards, unpunched, can go inside a package with the sender's greeting and name.

DECORATING PACKAGES

Pretty packages add much to the pleasure of opening gifts. If the gift looks tempting on the outside, you're sure it will be beautiful within!

The decorations on your packages can be kept intact if you wrap the boxes and their covers separately. On the cover paste cutouts to match the mood of the season —Christmas colors and designs for Christmas, angels and flowers for Easter and birthdays. You'll find cutouts that will be appropriate for almost every occasion on your Christmas cards.

2

The Party Table

THE SPOTLIGHT of most festivities shines on the party table—the dining table, the buffet, the supper table, the table that holds the punchbowl for the Christmas glug. Try trimming your table with some of your own creations. Here are a few suggestions to start you on your way.

TABLE TRIMS

Easy-to-make table and mantel trims can tell a story or simply add some color with a string of trees or candles. Small branches of evergreens can be used to complete the seasonal picture. Ring your punchbowl table with cutout trims and holly.

The base is made of a long strip of colored cardboard or construction paper—as long as you like. Figures cut from Christmas cards are pasted at even intervals along the inch-wide cardboard base. Then the base is folded at about 4-inch intervals in an accordion fold, so it will stand up in a zigzag manner.

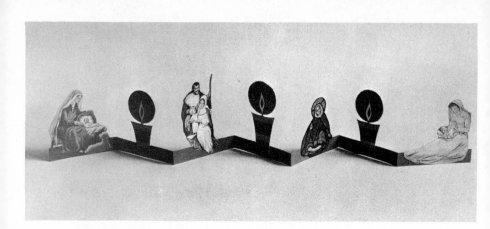

For birthday party table trims, use pastel colors for the base, and children or angels, or perhaps a series of toys or animals, for the cutouts. For Easter use angel cutouts.

FLOWER ARRANGEMENT PLACE CARDS

If you are planning a party luncheon, decorate your table with place cards of flower arrangements cut from Christmas cards. The assortment is surprising, once you start to look for them. Here we have copper containers, a willowware cup and saucer, a chafing dish and an elaborate brass scale. These would be especially appropriate for flower arranging friends. If your party is to include friends with mixed hobbies, you might find an appropriate cutout for each—a Santa putting for a golfer, or a skier for a ski enthusiast.

Each cutout is pasted to its own base, a little to left of center to leave room on the card for the guest's name. Directions for making the bases are given below.

BASES FOR CUTOUTS

Bases for Christmas card cutouts can be made of any lightweight cardboard or plain Christmas card. The base is an oblong shape, about 1 by 2½ inches, depending on the size of the cutout.

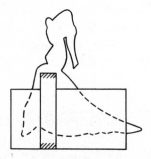

Place the cutout on the base about a quarter of an inch up from one long edge. On the back, paste a narrow strip of plain card to the bottom of the base and to the cutout, as shown by the shaded areas in the drawings. Let the glue dry for a moment, and then lift the cutout up as you pull the base down—and your figure will stand upright.

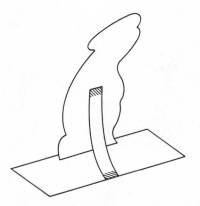

CHILDREN'S PLACE CARDS

These place cards are fine for children's parties all through the year, and they are simple to make. Plain white cards about 4 inches square are folded in half. Cutouts of children or animals are pasted to the cards so that the top part of the cutout stands above the folded edge (see photograph). When the cards are opened flat the figures should not extend beyond the square cards. This makes it possible to store them away in flat piles without crushing the cutouts.

Place cards of this sort make attractive gifts when packaged in sets of six or eight.

MAILBOX PLACE CARDS

Mailboxes cut from cards are glued to plain gold bases for place cards on the party table. Package them in sets of six for gifts or use them at your own party and write your guests' names right on the mailboxes. Directions for making the bases are given on page 28.

PARTY PLACE MATS

Place mats for parties—or for everyday use—can be colorful and practical and are easily made.

Choose your cutouts for color and design, so they will correspond with the rest of your table decorations. For the mat, use a piece of 12 by 15-inch construction paper of a color that also will go with your scheme of

decor. Plan the arrangement on the mat carefully. When you are satisfied with the design, paste the cutouts in place with very small dots of Sobo or any other white glue.

Cover the mat with a 12 by 15-inch piece of clear Con-Tact, and your place mat will last for many parties —just sponge it off after each use.

For children's birthday parties, make smaller place mats, about 9 by 12 inches. Use pastel-colored paper and cutouts of angels, animals, or toys. For a design of

a birthday cake in the center of the place mat, as shown here, use an oval-shaped lace paper doily, or cut a round one in half, snip away about an inch from the straight edge of each half, and then fit the two halves together again. This gives an elliptical shape. Around the "birthday cake" paste pastel-colored candles cut from Christmas cards. And around the place mat, to set off the cake, paste pink and blue angels, if the party is for a little girl. If it is a boy's party, paste animal cutouts around the cake.

PARTY COASTERS

Useful as well as decorative, these coasters will give perfect protection for your finest furniture. They are so easy to make you can put them together for one special party. But they are so sturdy they will last indefinitely.

Start with a plastic coffee can top (the standard size is 4 inches across, just right to hold a glass). Cover the rim of the plastic top with Mystic Tape or Con-Tact Tape (both kinds are self-adhesive) in red, green or gold color. I like to cover the outside edge first and then fold the tape over the rim and down into the inside of the lid.

Next, cut a 4-inch circle from one of your cards, either a plain color or gold or silver, or an over-all design of many colors. Glue the circle to the inside of the plastic top with Sobo glue.

If you use a plain color for the inside of your coaster, cut out a Christmas wreath from one of your Christmas cards (silhouette the wreath completely, so that none

of the background of the card is left) and paste it in the center of the coaster. Choose your colors carefully—a red rim with a red and gold wreath, a wreath of many colors with a plain green background and rim, an all-gold wreath on an all-green coaster.

Instead of trimming the rim of the coaster with tape, you can glue narrow satin ribbon around the edge, both inside and out, and finish with a tiny bow.

If you want to keep your coasters for a very long time, cut a 4-inch circle of clear Con-Tact (it is self-adhesive) and place it over your completed design. This will protect your cutouts from the drips and drops of many glasses. And you can wipe off your coaster with a damp cloth after every party.

3

For Doors and Walls

IF YOUR DOORWAY is decorated, all your friends know that the holiday spirit has come to your house. And if your doorway is protected so the winter winds, the snow and rain won't strike it, you can use a decoration made from your Christmas cards.

Inside doors, too, can be decorated—the hall door, the kitchen door and the doorway to the den. For these doors, and also for walls, you can make swags, posters, and panels, some of seasonal colors, some that tell stories, and some that simply give a lift to your everyday decor.

KLOCKASTRANG CHRISTMAS TREE

A klockasträng in Scandinavia is a door decoration for holiday time that usually has a bell attached to it somewhere, so it can be used to announce the arrival of visitors. This klockasträng, in the shape of a Christmas tree, has no bell, but it does decorate the door—either an inside or a protected porch door—for the holidays.

Almost as much fun to decorate as a real Christmas tree, this tree takes time and patience and a search through the Christmas cards. But when it is finished it is bright and colorful and sparkling, and everyone knows that Christmas is near when it is hung upon the door.

I started with a pattern cut from a newspaper (I cut several until I was satisfied with the shape). Then I traced the pattern on a 12 by 18-inch piece of dark green construction paper, and cut out the tree. Next, I trimmed off about three-quarters of an inch of the newspaper pattern—all the way around but not the bottom—and traced around that on a piece of lighter green construction paper. I then pasted the smaller light green tree upon the larger dark green tree.

From my collection of Christmas cards I cut all kinds of decorations, including lighted candles, large and small, tiny Christmas tree balls, stars sparkled with glitter, and a few candles surrounded by evergreens.

Before securing the decorations to the tree with a drop of Sobo glue, I made quite sure they were placed where I wanted them, changing and arranging by color and by size. When they were exactly as I wanted them, I pasted them down and hung the tree (using double-faced Scotch tape) upon the front door to welcome in the season.

KLOCKASTRÄNG OF BELLS

A cluster of bells for your doorway rings in the Christmas season. This klockasträng goes on an inside door, where it will be protected from the wintry weather.

Each bell is made from a half-circle cut from a plain card. Use red, green, blue, and gold or silver, mixing the colors for the best effect.

Form a cone of the half-circle and fasten with glue.

Run a narrow red satin ribbon up through the point of
the cone and secure with a drop of Sobo or Elmer's
glue. Knot the ends of the ribbons together, arranging
the bells at varying lengths, and attach with fine wire to
a branch of evergreens. Tie with a wide red satin bow
and hang on your door.

POINSETTIA PANEL

An assortment of poinsettia blossoms cut from Christmas cards and pasted to a 12 by 18-inch piece of construction paper (I used chartreuse-colored paper) makes a colorful and appealing decoration for your wall, or for an inside doorway.

Even though the poinsettias in mine were cut from seven different cards, the colors and designs of the flowers blend well together. I found enough variation in size and in shading to make an interesting arrangement, with the darker shades at the bottom, the lightest at the top of the panel.

Make your entire arrangement before you begin to paste. Try it several different ways until it is just as you want it to be. Then tack the cutouts to the background with Sobo glue. Hang on wall or door with double-faced gummed tape.

POSTER OF BIRDS

For a bright decoration to hang on wall or door during the holidays—or at any time—paste up a poster of birds and branches.

I made mine on a 12 by 18-inch piece of light blue construction paper. The birds and branches and the bird feeder were all cut from Christmas cards—four different ones. The branches were cut apart and rearranged for the sake of good panel design. The cardinal at the left, for instance, sits on a long branch that was formed when a piece of the lowest branch was cut off and pasted at the top, behind the bird.

Fasten the cutouts to the background with small dots of Sobo glue, and attach panel to door or wall with double-faced gummed tape. Be sure it is an inside door, for the panel will not withstand rain and snow.

LITTLE RED RIDINGHOOD

Pictures for the children's room can tell their favorite stories. Here Red Ridinghood is hurrying through the woods to Grandmother's house (a cookie house with a candy-cane chimney, cut from a child's Christmas card).

The wolf in this case turns out to be a fox, but it was the best the cards had to offer!

The cutouts are pasted on a piece of light blue construction paper measuring 9 by 12 inches. This in turn is pasted on a 14½-inch pale yellow sheet of construction paper, which provides a frame for the picture. A strip of double-faced gummed tape across the back, at the top, will hold the panel to the wall.

THE PIED PIPER

Your children can make their own wall decorations with cutouts and make up their own stories. Or they can make pictures of the oft-told tales.

Here the Pied Piper leads a long line of little children, diminishing in size to the last running figure, all leaving their little village behind. The card cutouts are pasted on dark green construction paper about 12 by 18 inches in size. Attach to wall or door with double-faced tape.

THE OLD WOMAN WHO LIVED IN A SHOE

Everything for this favorite nursery rhyme was found among Christmas cards except the shoe, which was cut freehand out of colored paper. All the noisy little children were found on one card, which was inscribed

Silent Night? The Old Woman, bringing home a basket-
ful of goodies, obviously smiles her way through life.
She was found on a card from Scandinavia.

I started with a piece of blue construction paper, about 9 by 14 inches, and arranged the cutouts around the shoe, which had been cut from a piece of chartreuse-colored paper. Shoe buttons were cut from a floral design on a card. Another card provided the windows and the little door in the toe, and finally a tiny ladder was found for the doorway.

Fido, the family pet, seems to be enjoying the whole scene, as the two birds sit quietly on a branch above.

After the figures were all pasted in place I mounted the panel on a chartreuse-colored 12 by 18-inch sheet of construction paper, which served as a frame.

4

Christmas Villages and Settings

MOST OF US LIKE to have a Christmas village to place under the tree or on a window sill or mantel. A quiet village scene symbolizes for us, perhaps, the spirit of peace that prevails at Christmastime.

Villages and crèches, and other seasonal scenes as well, can be made with Christmas cards.

THE CHRISTMAS VILLAGE (THREE-DIMENSIONAL)

The village that nestles at the foot of the Christmas tree is usually a snowy scene of houses and a barn, with a village church nearby. This village, under the tree, has three-dimensional buildings made from Christmas card cutouts. The little buildings are placed on cotton batting.

For a small hill, I placed an oblong-shaped cereal box under the "snow" so the church could look down on the rest of the town. Triangular trees made from cards (see Chapter VII for directions) stand guard by barn and houses. The trees by the church are cutouts pasted to their own bases (instructions for making the bases are given in Chapter II).

53

To the left of the church at the side of the hill is a fence cut from a card, leading from the hilltop to the field below. The lamppost stands on its own base, as does the village crier who is knee-deep in snow.

THREE-DIMENSIONAL BUILDINGS

It is so much fun to make three-dimensional buildings with cutouts that I usually find I have many more churches than I need for my village, and the streets can't accommodate all the little houses.

First I select a picture of a building that faces squarely forward. (Buildings that are partly turned to one side are better for the two-dimensional village.) Then I select a shade of construction paper that either matches or blends well with the cutout.

Next, I trace around the cutout on the construction paper. This makes the back wall of the building—it will exactly match the front. I leave enough paper to the right and to the left to form the side walls of the building.

If I am making a church, I do not trace around the steeple. I leave that two-dimensional, and trace only as far up as the top of the peaked façade. This gives the back wall of the church a matching peaked façade.

You must depend upon your own eye for the proportions of each building. For a church I usually make the side walls about one and a half times as long as the width of the front. On the other hand, if the front of the building is quite broad, then I make the side walls rather shallow. Again, it depends on your own sense of proportion.

After tracing around the cutout, I extend (using a ruler) the lines each side of the cutout to form the two side walls, plus about a quarter of an inch at both ends for pasting tabs. Then I cut out this shape, bend it to make side and back walls (the traced front becomes

the rear of the building), and then paste this frame to the front with the two quarter-inch tabs. This makes the building without its roof.

For the roof I cut a rectangular piece of the same paper as I used for the walls. The size of the roof is determined by the length of the side wall, and the length of the façade, including peak, if there is one. Fold the roof to fit *over* side walls and back wall and *against* the front wall. Secure roof to building with a few drops of Sobo glue.

If you are making a house that has a more complicated shape, follow the same steps. As long as your back wall (traced from the front of the house) matches the front, and the side walls are even, you can fit a roof across the top, no matter how many gables there are.

You'll find that the buildings are remarkably sturdy.

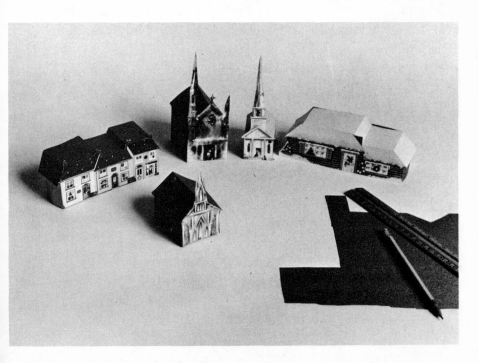

I've set up my village and packed it away many times without losing a single house or church or barn.

CHRISTMAS VILLAGE (TWO-DIMENSIONAL)

For my two-dimensional village I used cutouts of houses, barns, churches, and (even though they don't really belong in a village) a few city buildings. I ar-

ranged the village under the Christmas tree on a snowy slope.

The hill is built up with boxes and then covered with sheets of cotton batting. The city stands in the distance on the top of the hill. Down the slope the village houses, with a barn, are nestled into the snowy hillside. At the foot of the hill the white village church still has its windows lit as the sleigh full of churchgoers is driven away.

Off to the right is a cluster of barns, protected by three triangular trees.

All the cutouts stand on their own bases (directions for making the bases are given in Chapter II), which are tucked into openings in the cotton so they are completely covered with "snow."

SANTA CLAUS'S ORCHESTRA

An appealing holiday scene for the mantel, under the tree, or perhaps on the piano, especially if there are musicians in the family, is this orchestra made up of

cutouts playing almost as many different kinds of instruments as are found in the best of symphonies. And, as is usual in orchestras, they are arranged in sections— the strings, the woodwinds, and the percussion. The vocal soloist is being cued by the conductor.

Each cutout stands on its own base (see instructions in Chapter II). Thus the orchestra can be folded up and put away for another occasion. The cutouts' bases are white to match the floor of the stage.

For a backdrop I used two shades of blue construction paper, the darker color cut to represent draperies and pasted to the lighter paper. The backdrop is 18 inches long and 8 inches high, with 4 inches bent at each end to form the stage wings.

PARTRIDGES AND PEAR TREES

While two carolers sing the favorite "Twelve Days of Christmas," all the characters of the many verses come marching out of a forest of pear trees and partridges.

Each cutout is mounted on its own base (see Chapter II for instructions) so that the whole scene can be folded up and stored in an envelope for another time.

For a snowy scene on the mantel, the hall table, or as a centerpiece for the holiday buffet table, arrange the characters on a sheet of cotton about 12 inches wide and 18 inches long. Then use white cardboard for the bases of the figures.

FLAT-ROOFED CRÈCHE

For this crèche scene I used several shades of brown, orange, and gold, starting with a sandy-brown piece of construction paper about 12 by 18 inches for the flooring of the setting. Each cutout in the scene stands on its own base made of the same sandy-brown paper.

The shelter is made of three pieces of construction paper in three different colors. I started with a piece of 9 by 15-inch dark brown construction paper. I folded this piece of paper so it would form the roof, the back

wall, and the floor of the shelter. The roof is 5 inches from front to back; the back wall is 4½ inches high; and the floor is 5½ inches from front to back.

For added color I made the floor double, using orange-colored construction paper for the extra piece, a sort of wall-to-wall carpeting! And to give more color to the roof I added a piece of light brown paper, cut a little narrower than the roof, securing it with glue.

To give shape to the shelter I tapered the back wall from 9 inches wide at the top to 7 inches wide at the bottom.

The pillars are narrow strips of cardboard 6 inches long covered with gold beading cut from a Christmas card. These pillars are pasted to roof and floor, giving the crèche structural rigidity.

A star cut from a Christmas card is pasted to the edge of the roof. The Wise Men on their camels, the animals and the other figures of the Nativity scene all came from Christmas cards.

CRÈCHE WITH A PEAKED ROOF

This Nativity scene, for mantel, hall table or under the Christmas tree, has a little crèche with a peaked roof. All the figures for the scene were cut from Christmas cards and pasted to paper bases (see Chapter II for instructions for making bases). The scene is set on a piece of 12 by 18-inch purple construction paper. Bases for the figures are made of the same purple paper so they won't be very obvious.

The little crèche is made of purple construction paper cut according to the dimensions given in the drawing. Cut a separate piece of the purple paper 2½ inches

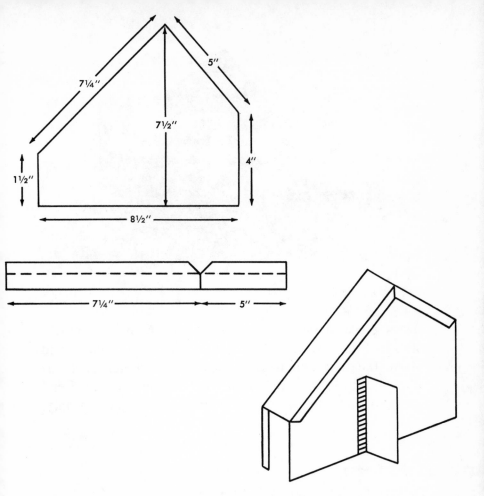

wide and 12¼ inches long for the roof. Make a half-inch notch 5 inches in from one end (and 7¼ inches in from the other). Fold along dotted lines as shown in sketch and paste to the crèche with Sobo glue.

The "beams" that hold up the roof at the front of the crèche are made of quarter-inch-wide strips of cardboard covered with strips of gold beading cut from a Christmas card. Beams are glued to the inside front edge of the roof.

To keep the crèche steady and help it to stand up,

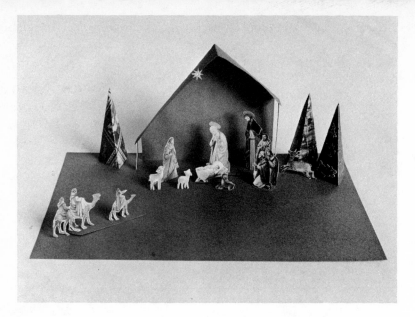

cut a piece of plain card, about 3 by 6 inches. Fold a half-inch in along the long side of the piece of card, and paste the half-inch folded edge to the center back, as shown in the sketch. (Paste the shaded area.) Bend card at right angle, and the crèche will stand firmly.

Table Trims

Tree Klockastrang

1

Poinsettia Panel

Bird Panel

Pied Piper

Three-dimensional Village ABOVE *and Two-dimensional Village* BELOW

Candle and Gold Angel

Old-fashioned Valentines

The Christmas Crèche

Snowman Maypole

Merry-go-round

Doll's House

Desert Scene

Old King Cole

The Candle Wreath

Santa's Orchestra

Partridge in a Pear Tree

5

Toys and Party Pieces

THE SEASON for children's parties lasts the whole year through, from Christmas to Valentine's Day and from Easter to Halloween. Here are a few suggestions for decorations and favors for children's parties, all made with the help of Christmas cards.

THE SNOWMAN MAYPOLE

Mixing up the seasons with complete aplomb, eight jolly snowmen wind their maypole of red ribbons in peppermint candy-stick fashion.

The base of this children's party centerpiece is made of a 16-inch circle of red Bristol board or cardboard. (Use a compass to draw your circle, or trace around a long-play record.) The circle is trimmed 2 inches in from the edge with a ring of lace cut from paper doilies.

The pole is a cardboard tube, 12 inches long, covered with white construction paper and wound with narrow (quarter-inch) red satin ribbon. Secure ribbon at top and bottom with Sobo. After the pole has been decorated, it is pasted to the center of the circular base.

Just a little Sobo will hold the maypole so securely that it will stand up perfectly.

To the top of the pole I glued a 4-inch circle of red construction paper. Spaced evenly around this circle I glued eight narrow red satin ribbons, each 15 inches long. Then around the edge I added a frill of lace cut from a paper doily.

To top off the maypole I made a cone of red construction paper, starting with a circle 6 inches in diameter. I slit the circle from one edge to the center point and formed a cone by overlapping the slit edges until the cone just fitted over the flat top without covering up the frill. This cone was then pasted to the flat top with Sobo.

The snowmen were cut from Christmas cards. Those that had writing on the reverse sides were faced with plain white pieces of card, so the maypole could be admired from all sides without any distracting lettering.

Each snowman was fitted into a small slit made in a colorful gumdrop—the large snowmen in so-called fruit slices, the little snowmen in rounded gumdrops. Then each snowman was placed upon the end of his own red ribbon. The weight of the gumdrops holds the ribbons, keeping the maypole strands in proper position.

CAROUSEL OF SLEIGHS

Even though the carousel is stationary, it appears to be whirling around, with its sleighs going full speed and its pennant flying. And it could be placed on a revolving cake plate, so that it would actually turn. This makes a fine centerpiece for a children's wintertime party. Various cutouts can be used instead of sleighs—for instance, animals, or just horses, or tiny automobiles.

The base of the carousel is a circle of green construction paper 12 inches in diameter. In the center of this base is glued a cardboard tube 9 inches long (from a roll of wax paper) that has been covered with green construction paper to match the base. A few drops of Sobo or Elmer's will secure the post perfectly.

The roof of the carousel is made of matching paper. I started with a circle about 11 inches in diameter, slit the circle from one edge to the center point, overlapped the slit edges to form a cone-shaped roof, securing it with a few drops of glue.

Around the circumference of the roof I pasted a scalloped edging about an inch wide. This edging is also made of matching paper. And in the center of the roof I glued a small strip of paper a quarter-inch wide to which was attached a paper pennant about 2½ inches long. The roof was then pasted to the top of the post.

The sleighs are card cutouts, and the trick is to find sleighs of about the same size, and of a size that will fit the carousel. I used five around my carousel, and I found four horses and riders to gallop around the center post.

The cutouts stand up, each on its own base of matching green construction paper (Chapter II gives directions for making the bases). The figures could be glued to the carousel, but I made mine on separate bases so they could be folded and put away for another time.

BIRTHDAY PARTY MERRY-GO-ROUND

A pink and white merry-go-round for the center of the birthday party table appeals especially to little girls. If it is placed on a revolving cake plate, the angels will really fly.

The base is a circle of pink construction paper 12 inches in diameter, edged with a ruffle cut from paper lace doilies and attached with glue. The center post, a 12-inch-long cardboard tube (from a roll of aluminum foil) is covered with pink construction paper and pasted to the center of the pink base. Sobo glue will hold it securely.

For the roof of the merry-go-round, cut a 12-inch circle of pink construction paper. Make a cut from the edge to the center point, slightly overlap the cut edges and form a cone—a very wide cone. Secure with glue. Trim the roof with a ruffle of white lace cut from paper doilies, and attach the lace loosely with tiny dots of glue. Fasten the roof to the center post with glue.

Seven angels cut from Christmas cards and backed with plain gold are suspended from the roof with black threads of varying lengths. As the backing is pasted to the angel the thread is placed between the two pieces of paper. Make sure the thread is placed so the angel will hang properly. Try it before you let the glue dry thoroughly. Then glue the end of the thread to the inside of the roof.

Toys and animals circle the base, all cut from Christmas cards and pasted to bases (see Chapter II for directions for making bases). A gingerbread boy and girl stand guard by the lion as Raggedy Ann watches the kittens and the rabbit dance.

PARTY FAVOR TREE

The next time you give the children a party, at Christmas or at any time of the year, make a Party Favor Tree for your centerpiece. (Some of my very young friends call it the Jelly Bean Tree.) Let each child choose his own favor to carry home after the party.

The tree is made of dried branches painted white or gold and fastened in a coffee can with plaster of Paris. The plaster is available at any hardware store and is easy to use. Just add water according to instructions on the bag, stand the branches in the mixture, hold them for a few moments until the plaster begins to set, and in ten minutes your tree is ready to trim.

Cover the coffee can with bright colored paper, using paste (or Con-Tact) and trim with gold beading cut from a Christmas card.

Decorate the tree with cornucopias made from Christmas cards, and fill the cornucopias with candy wrapped in bright tissue paper. The cornucopias are made of half-circles cut from cards. Use plain-colored cards or cards with an over-all pattern. Form a cone with the half-circle, fasten with glue. Punch a hole on each side of the cornucopia and run a red or gold cord through the holes for a handle. Make them ahead of time and stack them one inside the other so your party will be ready at a moment's notice.

THE DOLL'S HOUSE

Two shoeboxes covered with red construction paper and furnished with Christmas card cutouts make an intriguing doll's house. Make it with the help of your favorite little girl, or make as a gift for her.

Glue the two boxes together. For the peaked attic, cut two triangles out of the two box covers (see sketch) and paste them as shown on top of the house. Cover the peaks with a piece of cardboard (roughly 4 by 15 inches —shoeboxes vary in size) as a roof.

Line the walls and floors of the house with plain paper. I used white construction paper—white because the cutouts provide so much color. Cover the sides of the house and the attic façade with red construction paper, fastening it with Sobo or Elmer's glue. The roof is covered with gray construction paper that extends at the ends of the roof to make 1½-inch eaves.

For the chimney I used a piece of a red Christmas card. I folded it to form a square chimney (about 1½ inches square) glued it together, and then cut it at a slant on one side until it fitted the slant of the roof. Then I secured it to the roof with Sobo glue. No pasting tabs are necessary—the Sobo will hold a straight edge against a flat surface very securely.

The attic window was cut from a Christmas card. The shutters, left unpasted, can be bent out from the attic wall as though they had just been opened.

Upstairs in the living room the fireplace has a mirror over it in which the Christmas tree is reflected (all cut from cards). I pasted the fireplace against the wall but left the tree unpasted so it could stand at an angle in the corner of the room.

On the wall behind the piano a window is pasted to the wall, and on the side wall next to the piano is a gold-framed mirror. The candelabra stands on the piano.

There *had* to be a chandelier, and a careful search through my collection of Christmas cards turned up one of the right style and size. It is pasted on the ceiling near the front of the house, so that shadows show on the wall behind it.

Downstairs in the kitchen stockings are hung at the fireplace, ready for Christmas Eve, and an impatient infant looks to see if Santa Claus is coming. The kitchen table and chair are pasted to the wall under the window (also pasted to the wall). The pot-bellied stove stands out in the room, supported by a cardboard base.

Bases for all the cutouts of furniture and people are made of white cardboard (see Chapter II for instructions) so they will be as invisible as possible against the white floor.

To light the path for arriving guests, a lantern is attached to the outside wall of the house.

The hardest part of making a doll's house is to find cutouts of the right proportions. I found that I had many more pieces of furniture than I needed, some of the right size, some too large, and some too small. You may be tempted, as I was, to put in too many pieces. A little girl who came to visit me told me quite firmly that the house was too crowded. With her help I eliminated several pieces, and then she played with the doll's house contentedly for the rest of the afternoon.

ALPHABET BOOK

The elaborate lettering on greeting cards—some of it in gold or silver and some in colors and sparkles—can make a colorful ABC book for a five-year-old.

I started with two pieces of 9 by 12-inch construction paper, dark blue and light green. I folded them in half,

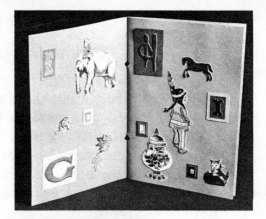

through the center of the longer side, and placed the green folded sheet inside the blue folded one. This gave me eight pages, with pages 6 by 9 inches in size.

I cut two notches on the folded edge of the book, through all eight pages, and ran a double strand of red yarn through the holes, thus making a binding for my book. The red yarn is tied into a bow at the center of the folded "spine."

To add color to the book, and to make the letters stand out against the page, I mounted each letter on a block of construction paper in a contrasting color and then mounted *that* on a slightly larger contrasting piece, with Sobo.

Starting off in the traditional way with A is for Apple, I soon discovered that some of the letters provided a challenge in searching for an object that would be suitable. Finding a queen for the "Q" and a valentine for the "V" wasn't so difficult, but I was completely bogged down with the "X" and finally decided to let it stand for Xmas.

DESERT SCENE

For a scene under the Christmas tree, for a children's party centerpiece, for a mantel decoration—dramatic settings like miniature stage scenes can be created from Christmas card cutouts, with the help of a little colored construction paper.

For this scene in a faraway desert I made an Arabian tent of yellow construction paper topped with a roof of orange. The "flooring" for the scene is a dark sand color, 12 by 15 inches in size.

For the tent I started with a circle 14 inches in diameter. Using only about one quarter of the circle, I made a cone 7 inches high. Leaving the cone unpasted—just holding it together, I pasted a quarter-inch strip of the same yellow paper around the outside of the peak of the cone 1 inch down from the point—a sort of collar to keep the tent closed at the top but letting the sides stay open. Then I snipped off the top inch of the point (above the collar).

For the roof of the tent I started with a circle 4 inches in diameter. I slit the circle from one edge to the center point, overlapped the slit edges slightly and pasted them together to form the cone-shaped roof. The roof was then pasted to the top of the tent with a few drops of Sobo, and one corner of the tent was turned back as a doorway.

The people, the animals, and the trees were cut from cards and mounted on bases. Directions for these bases are given in Chapter II.

To make the bases as invisible as possible, I used the same color of construction paper as that used for the foundation of the entire scene—a dark sand color.

OLD KING COLE

All the cutouts for the Jolly Old Soul were found on cards, except for the pipe. That was cut from a piece of plain gold card and given to a Santa Claus cutout to present to the King.

The musicians-three should, of course, all be fiddlers, but in this scene one of them is blowing a pipe and the other two are strumming on what appear to be mandolins.

The bowl that the white-bearded St. Nick is offering to the King is a bowl filled with fruit.

To give the King a royal setting I used a backdrop of

dark red construction paper 18 inches long and 12 inches high, with about 4 inches at each end bent forward and tapered at the top for stage wings. In the center of the backdrop is a golden garland cut from a card. The floor of the stage is a piece of purple construction paper, 12 by 18 inches in size, and the steps and platform upon which King Cole is standing are made of matching paper.

To the right of the King's platform stands a golden Christmas tree, and to the left a golden urn piled high with fruits and foliage of gold.

Each cutout stands on its own base (see Chapter II for directions), so the scene can be packed away and used again for another occasion. The bases are made

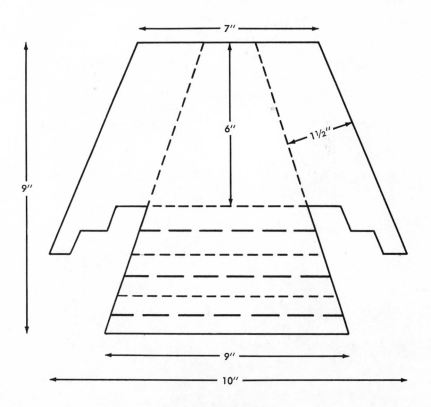

of purple to match the floor of Old King Cole's stage.

To make the platform and its flight of steps, start with a piece of purple construction paper 10 inches square. Cut it according to the diagram given. The platform is 6 inches long from the back edge to the top of the steps. Each fold of the steps is a half-inch wide. Each of the zigzag cuts of the sides of the platform are a half-inch long. Fold the steps along the dotted lines; fold down the sides of the platform along the dotted lines. Glue the sides of the platform to the ends of the steps, and stand your King upon his throne.

6

Advent Calendars and Cards

MAKING ONE'S OWN CARDS is always an adventure, especially for children. And making Advent calendars, with all their little windows and doors, is fun indeed when you have at hand a wealth of colors and designs to choose from. Your Christmas cards will provide all kinds of material for cards, calendars, and valentines.

SMALL ADVENT CALENDAR

A severely simple house, with trimmings in gold and red, makes this Advent calendar compact enough to stand on a mantel or hallway table, or to send through the mail as a Christmas card—a *big* Christmas card!

The house, cut from a piece of dark blue construction paper, is 13 inches high and 8½ inches wide. First, draw the house, including the chimney, on the blue paper, and cut it out. Then, with a ruler, draw 23 windows, one for every day from December 1 to 23. Arrange the windows as you like. Mine are about ¾-inch high and about as wide, except for the half-inch-

high ones just over the doorway. Next, draw a door for
December 24. Draw a line down through the center of
each window and through the center of the door.

Place the house on a piece of heavy cardboard, and
with a razor carefully slit across *top* and *bottom* and
down through the *middle* of each window and the door.
(Don't cut the sides!) Use a ruler edge to guide the
razor.

Bend back the shutters and trim them with strips of
beading and colorful designs cut from cards. I used gold
beading for the top two tiers of windows, then a row of
red shutters, a row of gold and then another row of red.
The door and the windows on each side of it are trimmed
with gold.

Wide gold beading (cut from the edges of a very large card) trims the gable and the chimney. Attach all beading with Sobo or Elmer's glue.

Next, trace around your house onto red shelf paper. Cut out the tracing and paste it to the back of your house (edges only) with the red side of the paper showing through the windows and door.

Each little window must have something in it, so cut out tiny figures—candles, an angel, a kitten, a sleigh—from your cards and paste one in each window. Inside the front door paste a little Christmas tree.

To make your Advent calendar stand up, cut a triangular-shaped piece of plain card, fold it a half-inch in along the long side of the triangle and paste this half-inch section to the back. Bend the triangle at right angles to the calendar.

Starting on December 1, one little window is opened each day. When December 24 comes, the door is opened —and there is the tree all ready for Christmas Eve.

When all the windows and the door are open, stand the calendar in front of a small lamp. Each little window will glow with the red of the shelf paper, and the Christmas tree in the doorway will stand out against the red. It will look like a house at nighttime, with all the lights turned on.

PINK AND WHITE ADVENT CALENDAR

This gingerbread house of pink and white has 23 windows and a big front door—an Advent calendar to hang on a wall. It is made exactly as the small Advent calendar is, except that white shelf paper is used. The

house, 19 inches tall and 9 inches wide across the bottom (it is a little wider at the top), is cut from pink construction paper and trimmed with strips of white and gold beading. The white front door has its own colorful Christmas wreath, and inside the partly open door can be seen the Christmas tree.

This house was suggested by a card showing the white front door with its wreath. The pink and white

house was built around the door. If you have a par-
ticularly appealing card of a doorway, choose your own
colors and make up your own design to go with that
doorway.

When the calendar is finished, attach it to wall or door
with double-faced gummed tape.

CHILDREN'S CHRISTMAS CARDS

Let the children make their own cards to send to their
friends from cutouts of last year's cards.

Cut out a Santa's head, a Christmas tree, a bell or a horse and rider—it should be fairly large. Then trace around the cutout onto the message part of another card—a message that has not been marred with handwriting—and cut out the tracing. Punch a hole at the top through both pieces, tie with red or gold cord, and your card is complete.

These cards can be hung on the Christmas tree, or if they are straight across the bottom they can stand on a mantel.

GOLD ANGEL CARD

If you have a large all-gold card and the sender's name is not written near the printed message, make a flying angel from the back half of the card. (The card must be gold on the *back*.)

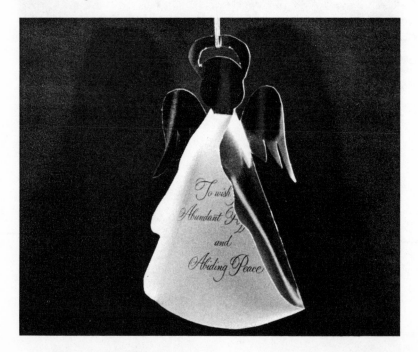

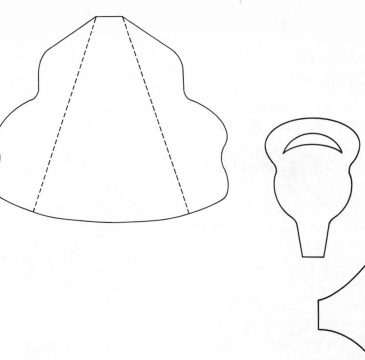

Following the sketch given here, draw the angel's robe, starting at the top of the card above the message. Fold along dotted lines, bringing the robe forward and enclosing the message. From another gold card (or the front part of the same card, if it is plain) make wings and a head with attached halo, according to the sketch. These pieces must be double, so they will be gold on both sides. Glue wings to back of robe, and head to front. Suspend the angel by a gold cord run through the halo. This card can be hung on the Christmas tree.

MOBILES WITH A MESSAGE

One way of making one's own cards from last year's cards is to cut out large letters from a message. Thread

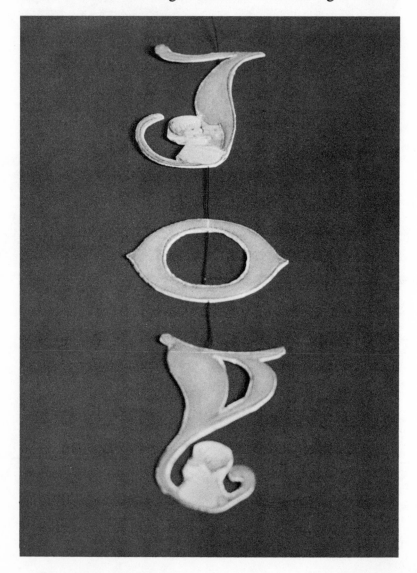

them together to make a mobile. Use NOEL, or GREET-
INGS, or CHEER, or MERRY CHRISTMAS, or other appropriate words.

Cut out the letters carefully, and then cut matching
shapes from a plain gold or plain-colored card. Arrange
the letters in a vertical row. Run a black thread up
through the center of each letter, starting at the bottom,
and leave enough extra thread at the top so the mobile
can be hung. With a tiny dot of glue place the matching
shapes on top of the thread. Write your message on the
plain side of the mobile.

OLD-FASHIONED VALENTINES

Valentines in three dimensions, decorated with lace
and angels, can be made from all-gold, all-silver or all-
red Christmas cards.

Cut off the back of an all-gold card, and use this for
your valentine. For the bottom cut an extra piece of gold
card about 2 inches wide to serve as a foot (see sketch).
Fold a half-inch as a tab and paste it to the back of the
card. With another plain gold card make a backing for
your valentine and glue it on. This will cover up the
message of the original Christmas card and also the
pasted area where the extra piece (the foot) has been
attached.

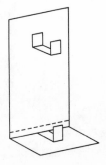

Decorate the front of your valentine with gold lace cut from cards or with lace paper doilies cut to fit. Add angels or flowers to your decorations.

Cut a frilly frame from one of your Christmas cards— you'll find several if you look for them. Make a tiny hinge of a strip of paper, about a quarter-inch by 1 inch, and bend it to form three sections (¼ by ½ by ¼). Attach the frame at the top to the valentine with this hinge (see sketch). This allows the frame to stand out from the valentine. At the bottom attach the frame with another hinge (folded a quarter-inch), this time pasting the hinge to the foot. The hinge lets the foot fold upward.

In front of the frame, again on a tiny hinge, fasten an angel to the foot and to the frame. The frame stands away from the valentine about a half-inch, and the angel stands away from the frame about a half-inch. When the foot is folded up the frame and angel move back and the valentine can be slipped flat into an envelope. When the foot is pulled down, the valentine opens up and stands by itself.

7

For the Coffee Table

JUST A SMALL TOUCH at Christmastime will create an atmosphere of festivity—a red candle with a sprig of holly, or a tiny tree on the coffee table. Here are some little additions for your Christmas decorations, and all of them are made with Christmas cards.

CANDLE RUFF

A ruffled collar for your candle will not only trim it up for the holiday table but will catch the wax drippings as well.

Using either a plain-colored card or one with a bright over-all pattern, cut a square about 3½ by 3½ inches. Fold in half. Cut slits along the folded edge to within a half-inch of the other edges (see sketch). Curl the ruff over a pencil—the card is quite stiff and if you don't curl the cuttings they will stand up straight. Wind the ruff around the base of your candle and insert in the candlestick. Use two or more of various colors for a fancier effect.

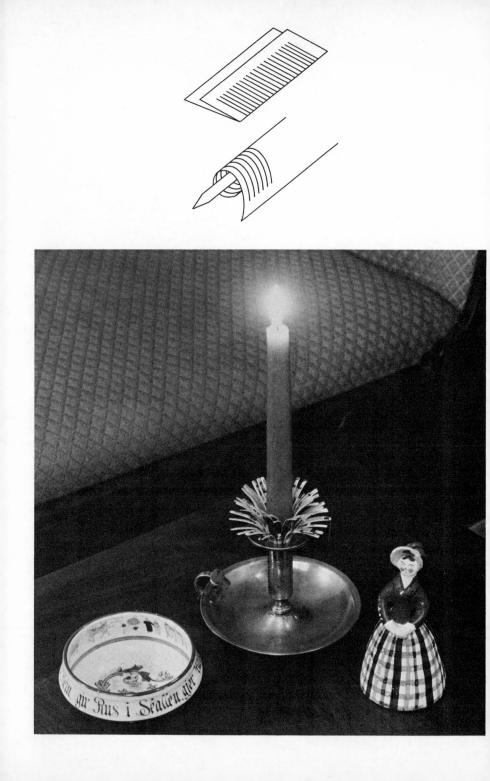

WREATH AROUND A CANDLE

Wreaths cut from Christmas cards make colorful decorations for candles, and they serve a useful purpose. They catch the candle wax as the candle burns down and protect the candlestick and the tabletop. Just cut out the wreath and slip it over the candle.

TRIANGLE TREES

To trim your Christmas village or to send as a holiday greeting, make a triangle tree. If you make several and want to keep them for another year store them with one stacked inside the other.

From a card with a bright over-all design cut the tree according to the diagram. Fold on dotted lines into

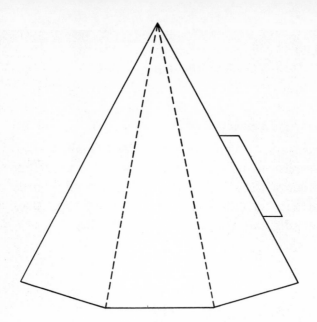

3 equal panels. Add a tab as in diagram. If you plan to mail the tree, leave it flat. The recipient can easily assemble it, either with a dab of paste or with cellophane tape. For your village paste the tree together.

If you use a plain gold or silver card, decorate the tree with small baubles cut from other cards.

CONE-SHAPED TABLE TREE

Trimmed like a Christmas tree, this cone-shaped tree will decorate your coffee table. It is about 9 inches high and is made of green construction paper.

Use about a quarter of a circle that is 18 inches in diameter (one circle will make four trees). Glue the quarter-circle to form a cone, and decorate with tiny Christmas tree trimmings cut from cards. Attach only the bottoms of the candles to the tree, and let the candles stand away from the cone, as they would on a real tree.

Slip a star into the point of the cone and secure it with a drop of glue.

Several of these cone trees will bring a sparkle to your Christmas party dining table, or to the Christmas Eve smörgåsbord table. Stand them on cotton to make a snowy scene.

HOLLY TREE

A cone-shaped holly tree made from your Christmas cards takes time but is effective as a centerpiece for a holiday party.

Cut a half-circle of stiff colored paper or cardboard 24 inches in diameter. Form a cone for the base of the tree, and paste it securely. I used a rosy-red construction

paper. My tree stands about 12 inches high and is about 6½ inches across the bottom.

Cut out (with manicure scissors) all the little bits and pieces of holly that you can find on your cards. You will end up with a collection of all shapes and sizes and colors of holly leaves, but when they are mixed together the effect will be lovely.

Paste the leaves to the cone, attaching in each case just a small part of the leaf, so that the finished tree will have leaves standing out from the cone base and will have the prickly look (and feel) of real holly.

GOLDEN ANGEL

A golden angel to stand on your coffee table at the holiday season is made from plain gold cards.

Cut a semi-circle as large as possible from the back of an all-gold card. Form a cone and fasten it together with paste. My cone stands 3½ inches high and was made from a 4 by 7-inch card.

From another gold card I cut wings and a head with attached halo (see sketch). I made the wings and head

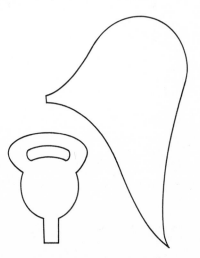

double, so they would be gold on both sides. The head was cut with a small tab that fitted into the top of the cone and fastened with glue. The wings were glued to the back of the angel. She stands on the coffee table and catches the glow of the candles.

8

Decorations That Hang

B AUBLES, BELLS, AND MOBILES to trim the Christmas tree, to hang at the top of the picture window, to suspend from the ceiling of the hallway where air currents are captured as friends come and go —all these can be made with Christmas cards, plus wire, thread, tissue paper, and paste. When the holidays are over, they can be packed away for another year.

THREE SOARING ANGELS

Three beautiful angels cut from Christmas cards, each one blowing a trumpet and each designed in bright colors that blend well together, are combined in a holiday mobile that floats gracefully from the ceiling of the entrance hallway.

This is one of the simplest forms of mobile—three figures suspended from two pieces of wire. The two larger angels are about 6 inches tall, the small one, at the top, is about 4½ inches. For these three figures I used one 7-inch-long wire and one 8-inch-long wire, all of it 18-gauge iron wire, available at most hardware stores. Each angel was backed with a piece of plain-colored card to hide any handwriting on the angel card. Between the two pieces of card a piece of black thread was inserted and fastened with glue. Before the glue dried I experimented to make sure the angel would hang as I wanted it to. A quarter-inch one way or the other can put a figure off balance. Enough thread was left at the top of the angel so the figure could be attached to the wire crosspiece.

The making of a mobile depends largely on balance. If you start at the bottom, balancing each section as you go along, your mobile will be successful. Each part should move freely, without bumping into another part. In this way the mobile creates a constantly changing, ever-intriguing, design made up of form and motion.

Starting with the shorter wire (7-inch), turn an "eye" under at each end. Long-nosed pliers are useful for this. To each of these eyes attach an angel by its thread (with a knot plus a drop of glue). I let the long, slender angel hang down farther than the one with wide wings, partly because of its slenderness and partly so the two angels could blow their trumpets toward each other.

Next, find the balance point of the crossarm. I do this by balancing the crossarm wire across my finger. In this case, the wide-winged angel was heavier than the slim one, so the balance point was off-center toward the larger angel. Using pliers, make a loop in the wire at that exact point, a loop that points upward. With pliers make sure that the eyes and the balance-point loop are parallel (when you pack it away it will lie flat in the box) and that the wire runs in a smooth arc from one angel to the other.

Make an eye at each end of the longer (8-inch) wire.

To one eye attach the smallest angel, and to the other eye attach a black thread that has been run through the balance-point loop of the first (7-inch) wire.

Again find the balance point, this time balancing the top (8-inch) wire across your finger. Turn a loop, straighten it with pliers, slip a black thread through it—and your mobile is ready to hang up.

MOBILE OF SWAGS

Strings of bells tied with bows, horns tied with ribbon, and three swags of holly make up a mobile that, because of the unusual shapes and brilliant colors, creates a constantly changing pattern of motion.

The swags are cut from Christmas cards, and the mobile is made just as the mobile of soaring angels is constructed, except that four pieces of wire are used instead of two. The cutouts vary in length from 3 to 7 inches.

The wires are 4½, 5½, 7 and 9 inches long. This mobile requires a rather large space, for when it is at its widest position, with all crossarms extended as far as they will go, it measures about 18 inches.

THREE-DIMENSIONAL TREE TRIMMINGS

Many colorful designs of bells and baubles found on Christmas cards can be made into Christmas tree trimmings very easily.

First, cut out the figure, silhouetting it completely. Next, trace around the figure onto a package of tissue paper that has been opened up but *not* been unfolded. Make your tracing on the top sheet of the whole package. Draw a line down through the center of the tracing, and along this center line staple two or three times. Be sure not to cut out your figure *before* you staple, or the pieces will scatter and you'll never get them back together again.

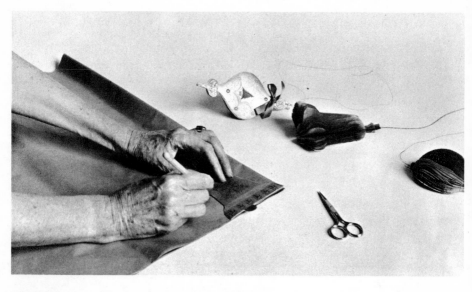

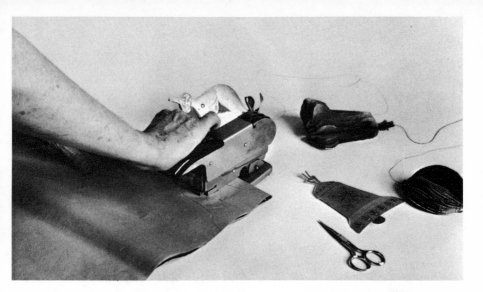

After you have stapled, cut out the figure, cutting through all thicknesses of the package of tissue paper. Cover the back of the card cutout with paste, and paste the stapled tracing to the cutout.

Then, leaf by leaf, unfold the tissue paper, creasing it along the center where it has been stapled. The leaves will stay open, giving you a rounded bell.

Attach a thread through the top, and hang the bauble on the Christmas tree.

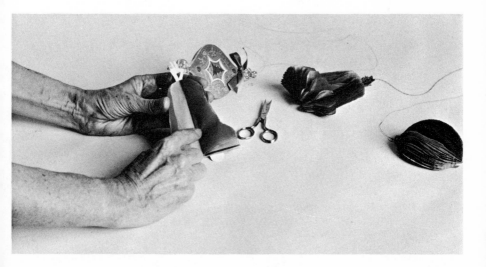

CHANDELIER MOBILE

The chandelier mobile lights up only by reflections, as the gold of its bells picks up the candlelight of the party table.

Three gold bells cut from plain cards are trimmed with red tissue paper, which makes them three-dimensional. Directions are given above.

The three bells are suspended at equal intervals from a 5-inch embroidery hoop that has been covered with narrow red velvet ribbon. Ribbon is pasted on. The hoop is suspended by three narrow red velvet ribbons that are attached to the hoop at the points where the bells are attached. A bow joins the three ribbons together, and from the bow a single ribbon suspends the whole chandelier.

MOBILE IN THE ROUND

Especially for the children, the Christmas tree mobile follows a popular Scandinavian design. A Santa Claus, a snowman, and four little children dance around the Christmas tree.

The figures were cut from cards and then were backed with cards of plain colors. A black thread was inserted vertically between the two pieces of card and secured with a touch of glue. Enough thread was left at the top of each figure so it could be hung from a wire.

The mobile takes three pieces of wire, each 9 inches long. The Santa and the snowman are hung from the ends of one wire. (Tie the thread to the wire and fasten with a dot of glue.) The four children are hung from the ends of the other two pieces. With long-nosed pliers, take hold of all three wires together at the center point and turn a loop. Twist the loop twice around, so the wires will stay in place. You now have an umbrella-like shape, with a cutout hanging from each "rib."

A Christmas tree cutout, backed with a plain gold
card, is hung from the center loop by a black thread.
Slip another thread through the center loop, and use
this to hang up the mobile. The children and Santa and
the snowman will dance around the tree.

BIRD MOBILE

Four bright green birds, all from the same Christmas
card, fly in fixed formation, because the separate sections
of this mobile are connected with wire instead of thread.
Each bird, however, is attached to the wire by thread.

The birds are backed with plain gold cut from other

cards. A black thread is fastened between the two pieces of card with glue. I found I had to experiment with the placing of the thread, so the birds would fly properly— if the thread is placed too far forward the tail falls downward; if it is too far back, the bird's beak dips down. Each bird is about 3 inches long.

For the crossarms I used three pieces of wire, one 6, one 8 and one 10 inches long. Starting with the 8-inch piece, for the bottom crossarm, I turned an "eye" under at each end, attached a bird to each eye, turned a loop at the balance point, just as for the angel mobile.

Next, I turned under an eye at each end of the smallest (6-inch) wire, attached a bird to one end, and at-

tached the bottom section of the mobile by its balance-
point loop to the eye at the other end of the 6-inch wire.
Thus, the middle crossarm (see photograph) is kept at
right angles to the bottom crossarm.

To find the balance point of the middle crossarm,
balance the wire across your finger. Turn a loop and
straighten it with pliers.

The longest wire (10-inch) forms the top crossarm.
Turn an eye at each end, attach the last bird to one
end and the balance-point loop of the middle crossarm
to the other. Tighten the eyes with pliers.

Once more find the balance point, this time in the top
crossarm. Turn a loop, slip a thread through it, and hang
up the mobile. You'll find that the top and bottom crossarms will face north and south while the middle one
faces east and west (more or less!).

FIVE FLYING ANGELS

The five flying angels of this mobile were cut from
plain cards—dark blue, gold, silver, green and red. They
are about 3 inches high.

To get the pattern for the angels, I drew a square
about 4 by 4 inches, on a piece of plain scrap paper, and
then filled in the square with a head with halo attached,
a flowing robe (which was almost a triangle, starting
at the neck) and wings. I chose a square to start with
because so many cards are that shape, or almost so, and
I wanted to make the most of the material that was available in the cards.

After I had sketched an angel that suited me, I cut

out the pattern, traced around it onto the five cards I had
selected, cut these out and backed them with plain gold
cards. As I pasted the angel and its gold backing together I slipped in a black thread so I could suspend the
angel from the wire of the mobile.

The mobile is made just as the bird mobile is, except
that there is one more figure—and therefore one more
crossarm. The wires for this one are, from bottom to top,
7, 6, 5, and 4 inches long.

The angels, too, fly in fixed formation, and fit nicely
beside a window because at their widest spread they take
only about 10 inches.

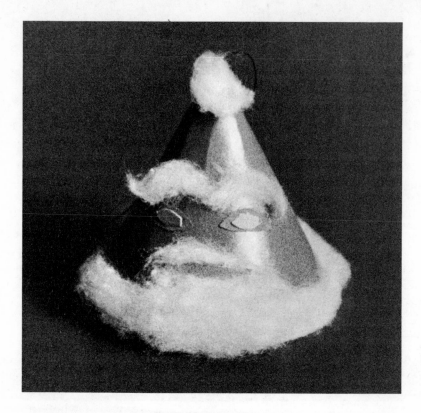

CONE-SHAPED SANTA

Hang a bright red Santa Claus on your tree. You can make it from one of your plain red cards.

Cut a half-circle as large as you can from the plain card. My circle was 3 inches in diameter. Form a cone and fasten with glue. Around the edge of the cone paste on a strip of cotton batting. For eyes and mouth cut pieces of dark blue or green card and paste in place. Make a mustache, wispy eyebrows, and a pompon for the top of his hat of cotton, and secure with Sobo. Run a black thread through the point of the cone, fasten with glue, and hang the Santa on the Christmas tree.

SOURCES FOR MATERIALS

The materials suggested are all readily available, either in five-and-ten-cent stores, hardware stores, or in art supply shops. Stationery shops, too, carry many different kinds of paper and glue.

For use with paper I have found Sobo glue and Elmer's glue invaluable. Both kinds are white when applied but turn clear when they dry, so they are almost invisible. And they both will fasten paper together, even edge to edge, very securely. Any of the so-called white glues will work just as well.

The clear Con-Tact, which is used for the place mats, comes by the yard in five-and-tens and in hardware shops. It is easily peeled off the heavy backing and smoothed onto the place mat.

Construction paper comes in two sizes, 9 by 12 inches, and 12 by 18 inches, in mixed colors. The quality of the paper varies slightly from brand to brand; the heavier kind is the easiest to use.

Small cans of spray paint are now available—one need not buy a huge can for a small job. When you use spray paint you must make sure your room has good ventilation. If you prefer to brush it on, you can get very small cans of paint in all colors and gold and silver. Small paint brushes, too, are available and very inexpensive.

Double-faced Scotch tape is now easily found, as is the so-called invisible Scotch tape, the kind that is slightly cloudy rather than shiny. All three kinds are useful for different kinds of jobs.

The wire I used for mobiles is 18-gauge, either copper or the ordinary iron wire. Both are available at hardware stores and at five-and-ten-cent stores. There is enough for several mobiles wound on the cardboard squares one finds in these shops.

Index

123